We were there

THE

1930s

Rosemary Rees

Heinemann Library,
an imprint of Heinemann Publishers (Oxford) Ltd,
Halley Court, Jordan Hill, Oxford, OX2 8EJ

OXFORD LONDON EDINBURGH
MADRID PARIS ATHENS BOLOGNA
MELBOURNE SYDNEY AUCKLAND
SINGAPORE TOKYO IBADAN
NAIROBI GABORONE HARARE
PORTSMOUTH NH (USA)

© Heinemann Library 1993

First published 1993
93 94 95 96 10 9 8 7 6 5 4 3 2 1

British Library Cataloguing in Publication Data
is available on request from the British Library.

ISBN 0 431 07331 7

Designed by Philip Parkhouse
Printed and bound in China

Acknowledgements
The author and publisher would like to thank the following
for permission to reproduce photographs:
Beamish, The North of England Open Air Museum: pp. 8, 13
British Film Institute: p. 21
Cheltenham Ladies College: p. 14
Con Dawson: pp. 25, 29
Hulton Deutsch Collection: pp. 11, 16, 18, 19, 23, 24, 30
Popperfoto: pp. 10, 26; Philip Parkhouse: p. 4
Robert Opie Collection: pp. 7, 22
Topham Picture Library: pp. 9, 12, 17, 20, 27, 28
Watts Publishing Group: p. 6
Cover photograph: Hulton Picture Company

The author and publisher would like to thank all of the people who
contributed memories for this book.
Joyce Skinner's memories are adapted, with the kind permission of the
authors and publisher, from *Growing up Downhill: A Book for Claire*, by Joyce
Skinner and Edna Purchase, Richard Kay Publications, 1989.

Note to the reader

In this book there are some words in the text
which are printed in **bold type**. This shows that
the words are listed in the glossary on page 31.
The glossary gives a brief explanation of words
that may be new to you.

Contents

Home 1

In the 1930s new houses like these were built outside large cities. Most people, however, lived in older, different houses.

Kathleen Galpin, when she was a child living near the village of Tolpuddle, in Dorset.

We lived on a **remote** farm in the heart of Dorset. We had plenty of good food because there were lots of rabbits, chickens, fresh fruit. There was no gas or electricity. Water was pumped from a well and it was very cold. We didn't have a bathroom and the toilet was outside. At washing up time, the first to get there bolted the door and stayed put until the dishes were done.

Bath night was quite an experience. A large tin bath was brought in from the garden shed and put in front of a huge log fire. Water was heated up on the stove in kettles and saucepans, and poured into the tin bath. It had to be kept topped up so that the last child still had hot water to bath in.

We never locked our doors and windows. We played all day in the fields and woods. It was all very safe.

This photograph shows a dolly tub on the left, and a posser on the right. They were used for washing sheets and towels.

Joyce Skinner, when she was a girl living in the city of Lincoln.
The washing was done in the wash house at the bottom of the garden. It was brick built with a slate roof, a tiled floor and a cold water tap over a channel that led to an outside drain.

Father filled the copper boiler with cold water on Sunday, and lit a fire under it on Monday morning before going to work. Mother began washing as soon as the water was hot. She washed small items by hand in a bowl, using a bar of hard yellow soap. She scrubbed dirty items, like shirts and kitchen towels, on a scrubbing board and then boiled them in the copper for twenty minutes. She soaped the sheets and put them in the dolly tub where she beat them with a wooden 'posser' She then boiled them in the copper. After twenty minutes she put them in a large bowl and rinsed them in clear water. There was so much boiling to be done that later loads waited until we were eating our dinner.

Home 2

Wives. Be Proud of Your Pastry! SEE BELOW

Wife and Home 6d MONTHLY

JUNE 1933

Simple Guide to PASTRY MAKING INSIDE

INTIMATE • INSTRUCTIVE • ENTERTAINING

Women's magazines like this suggested ways on how to look after the home and children.

Chris Walker, when he was a boy living in Cumbria.

We had a coal fire which heated the oven for baking all the bread, pasties and cakes – all home-made.

My mother made bread one day, cakes and pasties on other days. Fourteen pounds of flour made enough bread for a week.

We didn't have a cooker. Mother did all the other cooking on a single gas ring. We had gas lighting downstairs, but used candles upstairs.

Peggy George, when she was a girl living in south Wales.

In September we picked blackberries from bushes on rough ground near home. My mother made blackberry jelly from them. She boiled the berries and poured the liquid into a **muslin** square tied over a pan. All the juice drained through overnight, leaving the seeds and woody parts in the muslin. She reboiled the strained juice with sugar until it started to set. Then she poured it into jam jars.

Some people owned vacuum cleaners like the one in this advertisement.

Glenys Roberts, when she was a young woman living in Mountain Ash, south Wales.

I had a routine for cleaning that never changed from week to week. Mondays were washdays, even if it was pouring with rain. On Tuesdays I cleaned all the windows downstairs. I swept and dusted the **parlour** and polished the furniture. Wednesdays were 'upstairs' days. I changed the sheets on the beds and swept, dusted and polished the bedrooms. Then I swept the stairs and hallway. Finally I scrubbed the pavement in front of the house. On Thursdays I washed the bed clothes. Then I cleaned all the brass and fire irons in the house. On Fridays I hung the kitchen mats over the line in the garden and beat them with a brush to get all the dust out. I scrubbed the kitchen lino, polished the kitchen furniture, swept the **scullery** yard and cleaned the outside toilet. Friday night was bath night so that we would all be clean for shopping on Saturday.

Home 3

Customers told the grocer, the butcher and the baker what they wanted to buy. Delivery boys then took the goods home for them.

Con Dawson, when she was a young woman living in Pinner, twenty miles from London.

If I was in the village, I told the butcher what I wanted and it was delivered the next day. Usually, however, the butcher's boy called every morning before 8 o'clock. He always came to the kitchen door. If I ordered some meat from him he was back with it by 10.30am. Once I ordered some **chuck steak**. When it came it had fat on it, so I told him to come back with a leaner piece. I was never sent chuck steak with fat on it again.

When I went to the grocer's shop I always chose the side of bacon from which I wanted the rashers cut. He cut them as thinly or as thickly as I wanted. If I bought things like tea, coffee, or sugar, the grocer weighed out the amount on some scales. He then twisted thick blue paper round his hand to make a cone into which he tipped the goods. The cones were very strong and never came undone!

Reg George, when he was a boy living in Barry, south Wales.

A trip to the grocer's shop was a great event. He rushed around at great speed, making sure we had exactly what we wanted. He cut great chunks of butter from a huge block. He slapped and patted the butter, using butter pats which were rather like small wooden spades, until it was the correct weight. He cut wedges from whole cheeses using a sharp wire – and always let me taste a bit first.

I loved shopping in the Co-op. When my mother paid for the goods she had bought, the shop assistant put the money and the bill in a small metal container which was attached to overhead wires. Then, at the pull of a handle, the container shot along to the centre of the shop where the cashier sat. She took the money and sent the container back along the wires to us with the change and a receipt. As a special treat I was sometimes allowed to pull the handle myself.

The shop assistant stood behind the counter and fetched everything the customer wanted. You did not help yourself as you do now.

School 1

Sometimes children played with hoops in the school playground. The hoops were made from wood.

Kathleen Galpin, when she was a child living near the village of Tolpuddle, in Dorset

We lived about two miles from the local village school. We had to walk to school every morning, and walk home again at tea-time. No parent had a car and there were no such things as school buses.

All the children in the whole school were taught in one long room. The children were divided into age groups, and each group had its own corner. At one end of the room was a large black boiler which burnt logs all through the winter. It had a fireguard around it to stop the children getting too close and burning themselves. On rainy days our clothes got wet when we walked to school. The teachers hung them over the fireguard to dry. They steamed gently all day and sometimes they smelled very odd. Everything was usually dry by the time we went home. If it was still raining our clothes got wet all over again.

Peggy George, when she was a child in Caerphilly, south Wales.

I first went to school in 1938 when I was five. I went to the Mill Road Infants School. On my first morning a teacher took me to a classroom and told me to sit at a table with three other children. In the corner was a rocking horse. Some children had rides on it. I did not. I found out later that the children who had a ride were the ones who had cried for their mothers. On Friday we were each given a toffee.

Doreen Thomas, when she was a child in Fforestfach, near Swansea in south Wales.

We wrote with old fashioned wooden school pens with metal nibs. Our fingers always got very inky. After a while, especially if you pressed hard, the nib would split, and shower ink everywhere. We then had to ask our teacher for a new nib. This usually made him cross. On Friday afternoons a monitor collected the **inkwells** and poured the ink back into a stone jar.

All children had to go to school until they were 14-years-old. This school was built in 1938.

School 2

Girls who did not go on to a high school were taught how to look after a home. These girls in Birmingham are learning about washday.

Joyce Skinner, when she was a girl living in Lincoln.

I went to the High School in the autumn of 1930. My shiny new leather satchel was stuffed with books. Many of them were new and all had my name in them. There were different coloured exercise books; a pencil case full of different coloured pencils, a ruler and a geometry set. I had a blue shoe bag to hang on my peg in the cloakroom with house shoes and gym shoes, all marked with my name.

My parents bought my uniform during the holidays. I had a blue felt hat with a green band and a badge on it, black stockings, navy blue knickers, white blouse, a navy blue tie, a winter coat, a navy blue blazer piped in green and a gym tunic. This was made from navy **serge** with three pleats in front and three behind, hanging from a velvet **yoke**. Its correct length was two inches above the floor when I was kneeling up straight!

In 1934 school milk was provided for children at one halfpenny for one third of a pint. From 1939 the milk was free.

Doreen Thomas, when she was a girl living in Fforestfach, near Swansea.

Some children were lucky enough to have milk every day. The milk came in little bottles with cardboard lids. There were no school dinners. We were allowed to take sandwiches for lunch, which we ate in the smelly cloakroom. Some children were always hungry. If a child took some fruit to eat at school a crowd gathered round waiting for the apple core or orange peel.

Rita Kay, when she was a girl living in West Hartlepool, County Durham.

My school took infants, juniors and seniors. The seniors' classrooms were upstairs. Each class had about forty children. They sat in double desks with iron frames. One or two children took the scholarship exam and went to the High School, but I didn't. I stayed at Jesmond Road school until I was fourteen and went to work in Marks and Spencers.

School 3

A display given by girls in High School to show what they had learned in their gym lessons. You can see their badges sewn onto the yoke of their gym tunics.

Joyce Skinner, when she was a girl in Lincoln.

At the High School those of us who had good posture (stood straight and walked well) were given a small red ribbon to stitch on the velvet yoke of our tunics. These were taken away if standards fell. I got one in my first year and nearly lost it in the Lower Fourth for leaning on a warm radiator. Each year the school gave small striped badges for skill in gymnastics. We had to stitch these onto our tunics, just above the red posture ribbon.

We played hockey and netball in the winter and tennis and rounders in the summer. For two years we played cricket. I played in the school first team for everything except tennis. I enjoyed all of it except for the bus travel when we had to go to other schools for 'away' matches. I always felt travel sick on the lumbering, green smelly buses that we hired from the Lincolnshire Road Car Company.

These boys played rugby on the school fields. After school, boys enjoyed going to their local fields to play football.

Jack Carpenter, when he was a boy in Islington, London.

As soon as tea was over, we boys would rush down to the local 'rec'. Its real name was 'recreation ground', but that seemed too posh a name for what was really a field of rough grass with some swings in one corner and some wooden seats round the edge. We always wanted to play football. It didn't seem to matter whether it was winter or summer. We marked the goal posts with piles of coats, jackets or jumpers.

We picked teams and began to play noisily. No one refereed: we sorted things out ourselves and anyone who disagreed was shouted down.

One year Billy's dad and my dad decided to take us in hand. They trained us and taught us how to pass the ball properly and how to shoot for goal accurately. We got so good that we played a match against the boys in the next street. We won 7–0 and were quite sure we were heading for **stardom**.

Work 1

Some men marched from Jarrow to London to let people know they were unemployed. They stopped at farms where meals were cooked for them on the way.

Roy Mann, when he was a boy living in London.

We were a family of eight: Mum, Dad, five sisters and myself. I suppose you could say we were poor. Dad's wages were £1 10s 0d a week. We all did what we could to earn a few pennies. My mother used to take in washing. This she took to the public baths, where there were huge washing troughs and ironing presses. She also used to do office cleaning at night – all to **supplement** Dad's wages.

I used to go to the local market on a Saturday to collect empty wooden boxes to break up and sell as firewood at one penny a bundle. I also used to help out on a fruit stall from about 9.00am to 6.00pm. My job, along with another boy, was to unwrap oranges. We used to put them in a sack and shake it backwards and forwards to remove the tissue paper from them. I gave the money I earned to my mother. She gave me back a halfpenny or a penny to spend.

Horses were used to plough fields. It was a very skilled job to keep the lines straight.

Ann Crane, when she was a child living in Diss, Norfolk.

We (my parents, two brothers and me) lived in a tied cottage. This meant that the cottage went with Dad's job. If he lost his job, we all lost our home. Dad worked for the local farmer as a general farm worker. This meant that he would turn his hand to anything: **hedging and ditching**, milking, haymaking – whatever had to be done, Dad would do it. He was best at ploughing.

I don't know how much he earned, but it can't have been a lot because we were always poor. Sometimes Dad went out **poaching** for rabbits, hares or a pheasant. Then Mum made a good stew and we ate well for days. But I was always afraid that Dad would be caught and **fined** or even sent to prison. He would certainly lose his job and we would all be thrown out of our home. Sometimes I was so sick with fear that I couldn't eat. But Dad was never caught!

Work 2

Some men worked in factories. These men made Morris cars in a factory in 1930. They added a different part to each car as it moved down the assembly line.

Roy Mann, when he was a young man in London.

I started work in 1938. I was fourteen years old and had just left school. I worked a 48-hour week and got paid 14 shillings. I bought my first suit for 25 shillings. I only wore it at weekends.

There was an aircraft factory at the end of our street. When war broke out in 1939 more planes were needed in a hurry. They took on more workers, including me. This was my first engineering job. I worked in the section of the factory that made bomb release gear. We were kept very busy with lots of government orders. One week in 1940 we were asked to do overtime. I couldn't work overtime because the law said I was too young. So my boss sacked me and gave my job to somebody older who could work overtime. I got another engineering job making **mortars** for **merchant ships**. I kept this job until I was called up to join the army in 1943.

Some women worked in offices like this one. Each typist had her own desk and typewriter.

Con Dawson, when she was a young woman living in London.

Before I got married I worked as a secretary in the London offices of the recording company HMV. My starting wage was £2 10s 0d a week. When we had worked for HMV for a year we were allowed two weeks' holiday with pay. Girls had to dress tidily. Men had to wear dark suits, black shoes and white shirts. On Saturdays they could wear sports jackets, grey trousers and brown shoes.

Lucy Holmes, when she was a young woman living in Staveley, Cumbria.

In 1934 Marks and Spencer advertised for staff for their new shop in Kendal. I applied and got a job. I worked there for seven years and really enjoyed it. There was a fresh fruit and vegetable counter where 20 oranges cost 1 shilling. There were HMV records for 1s 6d each. My starting wage was £1 5s 0d a week. By the time I left this had gone up to £3 10s 0d.

Spare Time 1

Children often played in the street. Sometimes they played a game of hopscotch.

Rita Kay, when she was a girl in Mountain Ash, south Wales.

My friends and I often played with our tops and whips in the street outside our houses. We chalked different coloured patterns onto the tops. When they spun they looked lovely. We played hide-and-seek and rounders. On dark nights in the winter we took turns to go to each others' houses. There we played board games like ludo, draughts, **halma** and snakes and ladders.

Glenys Roberts, when she was a girl in Mountain Ash, south Wales.

We used to go and try to get a long rope from the greengrocer. We wanted to use it for skipping. We tied one end to a lamp post or to an orange box. One of us held the other end and turned the rope. The idea was to get as many girls as possible jumping in the rope at the same time. We played whip and top too. The boys used to play football and **hook wheel**.

Most cinemas showed children's films as well as films for adults. These children are queuing to see one of their favourite films.

Kay Styles, when she was a girl living in Manchester.

Every Saturday we went to the local cinema. This cost us **tuppence** (2d) each. The programme had at least two cartoons, news and a serial. Every week the serial ended with the hero (usually *Flash Gordon*) in a very dangerous situation. We had to go back the following week to find out what happened! Afterwards, we rushed home playing detectives, or cowboys, or whatever we had been watching.

Ann Crane, when she was a girl living in Diss, Norfolk.

Near the farm where my father worked was a river which ran into a deep pool. When the weather was very hot all the local children used to swim there. No one had a swimsuit. We just stripped off down to our underpants or knickers and jumped in. The older children dived in where the water was very deep. No one taught us to swim – we just learned how to do it from the other children.

Spare Time 2

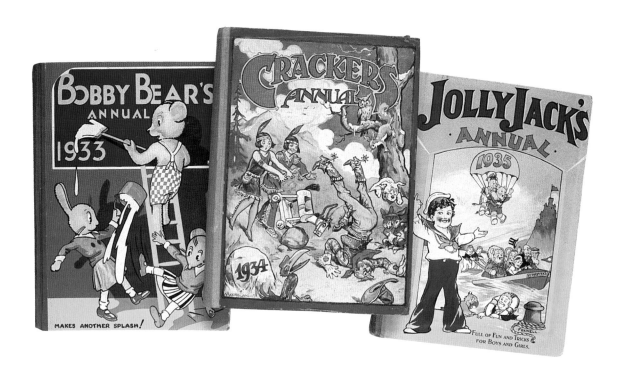

Children in the 1930s read comics. These are some of the annuals of the comics they read. Are they like the comics you have today?

Kay Styles, when she was a girl living in Manchester.

I loved going to the corner shop at the end of our street. It sold comics, newspapers and magazines, cigarettes and tobacco, wrapping paper, brown paper, string and all kinds of things. Best of all it sold sweets. As well as large jars holding things like jelly babies, aniseed balls and dolly mixtures, there was a halfpenny tray and a penny tray. On the halfpenny tray there were long strips of liquorice rolled round a sweet; gob stoppers which changed colour as you sucked them; tiny sticks of rock and sweets in bright wrappers. On the penny tray were sherbet dabs – a bag of sherbet with a flat sweet stuck on a stick which we licked to dab up the sherbet and twisty sticks of barley sugar. Behind the door of the shop was a rack which held newspapers at the top and comics at the bottom. If the shop was busy, you could read a whole comic while pretending to choose some sweets.

**This was a dance hall in Manchester in the 1930s.
The band played the music for people to dance to.**

**Con Dawson, when she was a
young woman living in London.**
I loved going dancing to the 'Big
Bands'. We danced waltzes, fox-trots,
one-steps and tangos. Some people
danced the 'Lambeth Walk'. Most
dances had what was called a 'Spot'
waltz. While we danced a huge silver
ball turned round on the ceiling. It
reflected spotlights on us all. When
the music stopped, the couple on
whom the main spotlight shone, won
a prize.

**Kay Styles, when she was a child
in Manchester.**
On Monday evenings our parents went
to the cinema. When Father's car
turned the corner, our sister lit the fire
in the sitting room. She sent us off to
bed, and invited her boyfriend in. My
brother and I were terrified our parents
would come home early and catch her.
They never did. Each week the
boyfriend went, the fire was cleaned
out and relaid, and our sister was
reading when they arrived home.

Holidays 1

This photograph was taken in 1935. It shows people enjoying their summer holiday on the beach at Southend, in Essex.

Glenys Roberts, when she was a child living in Mountain Ash, south Wales.

When I was a child we never went away on holiday. My parents couldn't afford to pay for us all to go to a **boarding-house** or hotel. For our holiday we went on an outing with all the adults and children from our Sunday School. Every year we went to Barry Island. We were so excited that we couldn't sleep the night before in case the train went without us.

Ann Crane, when she was a girl living in Diss, Norfolk.

The first summer holiday we had away from home was when we went to Butlin's holiday camp at Skegness. We went there by bus from Norwich. I can remember that the seats of the bus were very hard. They were covered in a scratchy fabric which made red bumps come up behind my knees. The first thing Mum did when we got to Skegness was to put **calamine lotion** on them.

These are photographs of Con Dawson and some of her friends and family on holiday in the 1930s.

Elsie Gardner, when she was a girl living in London, remembers the summers.

We often went to Eastbourne for a week during the summer holidays. We stayed in a boarding house. The landlady cooked us breakfast. We ate a picnic lunch on the beach and had fish and chips most nights.

We always played beach cricket and made sandcastles. Every summer we managed to bury Dad in the sand – except for his head!

Rita Kay, when she was a girl living in west Hartlepool, County Durham.

On Sundays in the summer our parents took us to the beach at Seaton Carew. There we met my aunts, uncles and cousins. The Dads built sandcastles while we children played leapfrog and the Mums knitted. At the end of the day we all played cricket. This all ended in 1939 when war broke out. Soldiers mined the beaches and spread coils of barbed wire over them.

Holidays 2

This is a photograph of busy Whitsun holiday traffic at Box Hill, Surrey, in May 1931. Whitsun is six weeks after Easter.

Vera Haigh, when she was a girl living in Oldham, Lancashire.
On Whit Friday father set off early to the Co-op bakery. He collected the specially made buns and took them to the Sunday School to be buttered.

We then rushed to meet the Barnsley band as it came marching up the hill. When the Band reached the Sunday School, we children were pushed into line by the ladies who had, by now, finished buttering the buns. We all set off in one enormous procession. We were led by the band and the adults who were carrying the huge Sunday School banner. We sang hymns outside cottages, houses, the Big House and the barn where our church started in 1672.

After what seemed to us to be a very long walk and far too many hymns, we arrived back at the Sunday School. There we had tea and buttered buns. When everyone had finished, we all went down to the Recreation ground for an afternoon of sports.

This family is having a camping holiday. They are stuffing straw into bags to make mattresses to sleep on.

Joe Scott, when he was a child living in Sheffield.

None of our friends at school in Sheffield ever went outside England for their holidays, but we were lucky. Every summer we went to stay on my uncle's farm in Ireland. There you got water from a pump in the yard, not from a tap. There was a **peat** fire with cooking pots hanging over it. The lavatory was a wooden earth **closet** next to the dung-heap in the yard. You soon got used to the smell! There was no electricity. After dark a **paraffin** lamp was lit in one corner of the kitchen, and you could read there. Most people sat round the fire, talking. You went to bed by candle light. There were calves to feed, eggs to collect and cows to bring in for milking. When Dick the cart-horse had to be taken off to the fields to graze, we were sometimes allowed to ride him. He never had a saddle on, but his back was very broad and we never fell off. For city children it was magic.

Special Days 1

These people were having a street party. They were celebrating the coronation of King George VI and Queen Elizabeth in May 1937.

Reg George, when he was a boy living in Barry, south Wales.

I was lucky enough to be staying in London with my parents in May 1937. On Coronation Day we got up early. We ate a big breakfast. I drank my tea from my Coronation mug for the first time. All children had been given a mug like mine so that they would remember Coronation Day 1937.

After breakfast we set off to get a good spot from which to see the Coronation procession. The streets were packed and everyone cheered when the King and Queen came past in their golden coach. I was on my father's shoulders, waving a flag and sucking 'gob-stoppers'.

Afterwards we went home and joined a tea-party in the street. We sat at **trestle tables** and ate cake and jelly. Next we had a firework display and sang songs until bedtime.

I am sure we enjoyed the day every bit as much as the royal family did!

This is a wedding photograph of Con and Ellis Dawson, with their parents, bridesmaids and best man. It was taken in July 1937.

Con Dawson remembers her wedding day in July 1937.

Every bride in my day tried to wear 'something old, something new, something borrowed and something blue'. My mother gave me a lace handkerchief that had belonged to her mother; I borrowed my sister Elsie's wedding veil; I wore a blue garter and my dress, of course, was new. It came from a shop called Bourne and Hollingsworth and I thought it was the height of fashion. My bouquet had red roses in it for love, and white heather for good luck.

After the wedding we had photographs taken. My mother sat next to me and Ellis's mother next to him. The two fathers stood behind their wives, with the best man in the middle and a bridesmaid on either end of the row. There were other photos of just Ellis and me. We went to the Conservative Club for the reception. All the guests were waiting. They stood up and clapped when we walked in.

Special Days 2

These people are having fun at a fairground. Their swing-boats are going higher and higher.

Frank Shuter remembers a travelling fair in Strood, Kent.

The fair came at the same time each year, about the middle of September. It was called the Hop Pickers' Fair because it came when hop picking finished.

The fair travelled from town to town. Some of the steam engines which powered the rides were also used to pull the wagons which the rides travelled on. Some of the people who worked on the fair had horse-drawn caravans. The fair travelled very slowly.

There were things you don't see now. My favourite was a boxing tent. There were two boxers who travelled round with the tent. We paid to go in and watch. People from the audience could fight the boxers. If they lasted two rounds they got £2. Hardly anybody ever did. There were roundabouts and swingboats and other big rides and lots of sideshows like hoopla, skittles and darts.

Glossary

boarding house private house, used as a hotel.

calamine lotion a liquid for soothing sore skin.

chuck steak beef cut from the shoulder area of a cow.

closet cupboard or very small shed.

fined having to pay money as a punishment.

fire irons metal tools used to tend a coal fire.

hedging and ditching make or repair ditches.

halma a board-game for two or four players.

inkwells pot for ink which sits in a hole in a desk.

merchant ships ships carrying goods for trading.

mortars cannon for firing explosives.

muslin finely woven cotton cloth.

parlour sitting-room.

peat rotten, decayed vegetable matter used for fuel.

poaching hunting animals and birds without permission.

remote situated away from towns and villages.

serge strong woollen cloth.

scullery small room next to the kitchen, for washing or storing.

stardom being famous.

supplement add to.

tuppence two old pennies (2d), now worth 1p.

yoke top section of a dress, from which the pleated skirt hangs.

Index